Blue Wren

For Saebah Rem. My sister, and my heart.
Together again and so proud of you living your truth and
being your dazzling, authentic self.

And for Jo. This simple acknowledgment cannot begin
to do justice to the ways in which your love sustains me
and keeps me focused. Your generosity and creativity
are at work in this collection, as well as in our beautifully
realised life together. You are my world.

Bron Bateman is a poet, academic and mother of nine. Her first poetry collection, *People from bones* (with Kelly Pilgrim) was published in 2002. Her PhD, exploring female embodiment and experiences of motherhood, sexuality, mental health and volitional marking through tattooing, piercing and BDSM practices, was completed in 2012. Her second collection, *Of Memory and Furniture,* was published in 2020 and was highly commended in the Victorian Premier's Prize for Literature in 2021. She has had her work published in journals such as *Southerly* and *Westerly,* and in journals and collections in the UK and the US. She has also performed her work locally, nationally and internationally. Bron received the Bobbie Cullen Memorial Prize for Poetry in 2004 and was awarded Columbia University's Winter Contest for Poetry in 2017. She lives with her wife and youngest daughter in Perth, Western Australia.

Blue Wren

Bron Bateman

▥ FREMANTLE PRESS

Contents

Fragment 7

Frida Kahlo

The Sticking Place 11
'Henry Ford Hospital' (1932) 13
'The Two Fridas' (1939) 15
'Self-Portrait with Thorn Necklace and Hummingbird' (1940) 16
'The Broken Column' (1944) 17
The Girl of My Eyes 19

The Girl of My Eyes

In the Dark 23
Hidey-Holes 24
To You 25
Kintsugi 26
On Saturday Afternoon 27
Orange Madonna 29
Sunday Evening 9.42 pm 30
Black, Black, Black 31

The Two Fridas

Eight Weeks 35
The Second 36
In the Beginning 37
Late 39
Little Bird 40
To Shrink Until I Am Small 41
Inheritance 42
A River in Your Hands 43
Blue Wren 45

Self-Portrait with Thorn Necklace and Hummingbird

At Four 49
At Seven 50
At Eight 51
At Nine 52

At Thirteen 53
At Sixteen 54
At Seventeen 55
At Twenty 56
At Twenty-four 57
At Twenty-eight 59
At Thirty-three 60
At Thirty-eight 61
At Forty 62
At Forty-five 63
At Fifty-two 64
At Fifty-four 67
At Fifty-six 68

The Broken Column

Petrichor: November 7, 2020 71
The Boys Who Dream of Winter 73
Tutankhamun's Box 75
In the Country 77
Sisters 78
Fourth Avenue 79
Ambitions 81
The Secret Sea 82
In Which a Universe Resides 83
So Beautiful 84
Crows on a Road Trip to Mount Barker 85
This Way Clad 86
Fishing with My Father, 1974 87
Circling 88
A Letter to My Mother 89
Metastases 90
Augury 91
Letters and Love Songs 92

Acknowledgements 94

Fragment

Cotton-mouthed,
I bite my lips
and tell the truth,
as much as I am able.

Frida Kahlo

The Sticking Place

At eighteen, on the way to Coyoacán
with your boyfriend Alejandro,
the bus you rode collided with a tram.

Your bones
s n a p p e d
like kindling,
your pelvis
impaled by an iron rail,

misplacing
your
spine.

I think of your thirty operations,
of your body encased, for nine months,
in plaster corsets.

In too much pain to study,
and pinned to your bed for all that time,

you borrowed paints from your father's studio.
Your mother had an easel made
and you began to paint.
Feet at first, but then self-portraits.

You said:
I paint myself because I am so often alone
and because I am the subject I know best.

I think of you, at eighteen,
already seeing the world
in crashes and grinding metal.
Layering your heart's blood onto the canvas.

'Henry Ford Hospital' (1932)

Here is a painting of you
haemorrhaging
on the hospital bed
like a bloody snow angel.
You started painting it nineteen days after
your second miscarriage.

Your body twisted in pain,
head and torso facing one way,
lower limbs the other.
An impossible contortion of flesh.

Diego will respond to this loss
by having an affair with your sister
—your best friend, your beloved little sister—

She, who should not have,
snared your husband so easily,
with her quieter, softer mouth
and her pretty, unscarred body,
while you bled and bled on the hospital bed.

The way he looks at her when he thinks
you're not watching
will catch in your flesh like thorns.
As you begin to recover,
he offers you squares of pressed tin to paint upon.

What can you do but colour your lips,
smoke another cigarette,
and paint? Your heart, this time:
as an open wound in your chest.
As a weeping eye raining tears of blood
onto your white frilly dress.
Or quivering like a timid bird
in the cage of your ribs.

'The Two Fridas' (1939)

With all the colour daubed on plaster and tin,
with all the colour swallowed over the years,
it is as if I have taken in the wholly lit moon and the sun
in one fearsome gulp.
I have bled you dry, my dear, other Frida, can you see the
little shocks of blood on our white lace dress?
Our one strong heart pounding truly in my open chest?

We are joined tenuously by a single artery,
a skein of memory, the connection of future and past,
the burden of family and loyalty running deep within us.
We love Diego. We hate Diego. We have left him in order to survive.
Our twinned bodies have both been rejected by him countless times.
We barely hold together. Heartbeats slowing
as I cautiously join our hands, entwining our fingers.
We are blood. A clotted dichotomy.
We shall endure.

Self-Portrait with Thorn Necklace and Hummingbird' (1940)

Diego gave you the spider monkey we see pulling
at the ends of the crown of thorns necklace.
The cruel spines pierce your skin,
beads of claret travel slowly down the column of your throat.
Black ropes of hair, piled on top of your head,
are studded with butterfly combs.

Two dragonflies hang pinned to a jungle sky.
A cat with ice-blue eyes curls against your shoulder.
To you he is like Diego, a symbol of the jaguar,
harbinger of chaos and death.
A dead hummingbird rests between your breasts,
the curve of its wings mirrored by the curve of your brows.

Your mouth, pain-stiff,
and slightly pursed, seems
about to sigh at us.
Your eyes, brown as pebbles,
stare unflinchingly from the canvas.
You dare us to wipe away the droplets of blood
gliding down your throat.
To pull at that thorny necklace
until you scream and scream and scream.

'The Broken Column' (1944)

In this painting,
with your torso splayed open,
you are a rejection of the boundaries
that separate human from animal
and human from machine.

The segmented plaster corset cuts into your ribcage.
Your spine is cast from iron,
and iron nails are hammered

into
your
flesh.

Slight oozes of red, flecks of sacrifice and death.

You paint yourself harsher and more unforgiving.
Your terracotta skin becomes
wide-pored and sallow,
your brows and moustache have grown thicker
with each passing year.

In another one of your paintings,
the little doe with the nine-pointed
antlers, and your face,
runs heedlessly into the woods,
blood streaming down its flanks,
its side punched full of arrows.

A hunting narrative emerges from the chaos:
An arrow's white vanes disappear into a deer's body,
forward and slightly low. The deer's hind legs kick out as it runs,
hard at first, then slowing to a staggered walk,
tail twitching erratically. Moments later it falls and lies motionless.
Solid evidence of at least one heart shot.

The Girl of My Eyes

Your hair, which you grow,
or cut short, depending on your mood,
is wrapped neatly around your skull.
He likes it long, and loose on your shoulders,
or piled intricately upon your head and woven with fresh flowers.

The painting of the two of you
shows you seeming to float,
inches above the ground,
tethered
only by the weight of his hand
holding you in place.
He, six-foot-tall
and three hundred pounds, in
brown shoes and his best grey suit.

He paints you and titles it *For the Girl of My Eyes.*
You are his wife and his muse.
He is the light of a Mexican summer
that washes you clean.
Your body is full of him
for days and days at a time.

The Girl of My Eyes

In the Dark

I met you in the dark,
you lit me up. All those times
I bit at your breast and shoulder,
stilling myself in the wrap of your arms.
The days where we looked at one another,
foreheads touching,
and it was enough; enough

to hold you close,
to calm you when you had nightmares,
to calm myself when I was barely
hanging on. When the heart
in my chest beat so fast it was as if I were
running,
helter-skelter,
from a hunter's gun.

When I look at you it's like looking into a mirror,
and swallowing my reflection.

I am Piscean,
golden flashing tails and writhing scales.
Hungry gasps of water.

Hidey-Holes

My lover is hidey-holes and carved doorways,
with her dark brown hair
rubbed satin between my fingertips.
My lover is wind chimes, plinking crazily adrift in a winter storm.
My lover is the best songs stolen from her Spotify playlist.
My lover is innumerable perfect gifts,
arriving in the mail from China, in small white parcels.
My lover is no held hands in public,
but gentle fingers at the nape of my neck
when no-one is watching.
My lover is a warm mouth pressed against my chest
and the lines of a new poem whispered in the darkness.
My lover is her midnight laugh.
My lover is spoken of in public.
No elision, or secrecy.
My lover is my wife.
My lover gave me our daughter.
My lover is an everyday act of rebellion.

To You

I love your mouth pressed carefully against mine,
your tongue, gentle, and seeking entry,
your fingertips circling my nipples; me,
riding your thigh as we rock to a rhythm
we have perfected over the years,
your words swirling through
my head, simple, and entreating.

But, perhaps best of all,
I love it when I hook my hands
around the tops of your thighs,
and spread you wide open,
thinking of summer fruit,
of nights fragrant with jasmine and musk,
of a breeze so faint
that the hairs on my arms shiver.

I know you prefer me not to write about this,
but when you asked me what I liked best,
I had all my answers ready for you,
counting them off on my fingers, one by one
as I shuck my skin and let you roam inside.

Kintsugi

A response to 'Ishmael' by Randolph Stow

I leave our bed to go to the toilet
in the chilly winter air.
I am tired and sated as I pee and wipe myself
with care, my vulva tender from having you inside me.
I mouth your sweet name, over and over,
like the words of a song I know off by heart.

After all these years together
our bodies are still a miracle to me. Making love,
the soft   O   of your mouth
against my skin, uttering fragments of nonsense
as I pull you in, the silken scissors
of my legs around your waist,
my ankles hooked in the small of your back,
your voice and my voice, both,
caressing one another.

I return to the bed,
where I open to every
curve and dip and press of you.
Your hand against my chest, I
pepper it with kisses, cradle it tenderly,
then open my mouth against your neck,
lap at the cooling salt of your skin.

On Saturday Afternoon

You lie, sprawled carelessly on the bed,
legs splayed, soft curl of fists by your side,
breath slow and unfurling from your chest.
Your breasts rise and fall
in my line of sight, your eyes are shut tight.

I flex my hand,
open,
shut,
open,
a clicking in my sore wrist

fingers stretched stiff, then carefully closed,
drizzled with lube that
drips onto the hotel sheet,
a warm shiny slide on my skin. I

breach you slowly
press,
press in,

twisting one way and then the other,
as I pause to tickle the soft rim of your cervix
with the tips of my fingers.
My bracelets jangle.
There is pain in my bad shoulder,
as I try to hold myself still,
so you can take all of me,
my hand and wrist enveloped
by your thick, blood warmth.
My fingers buzz and tingle.

You moan. That beautiful sound.
Then we are both silent.
Nothing but breath.
Nothing we can say at this moment
that's worth a damn.

The harsh yellow light makes pinpricks of my pupils.

Inside you past the second fold on my wrist,
fucking you with my fist
surer and with more certainty,
than any cock could.

Orange Madonna

For Jo

I watch the way you cut orange and lemon segments,
the snick of the knife on the chopping board,
the flick and stress of your brown wrist.
Most of the time you are too uncomfortable in your body
to realise how lovely you are to me.
It is only in these moments, with your face grave and tender
as you navigate around the baby at your feet,
telling me about your day, asking about mine,
that you settle into yourself,
loosen the strings that hold your shoulders tight
and dance your fingers across the pieces of fruit in front of you.

Sunday Evening 9.42 pm

You are so clever with me, I can hardly believe it,
with your downturned eyes, your palms,
warm and certain on my shoulders, the tip of
your tongue tracing thirsty circles on my neck.
Today, I stood in front of you,
took your face in my hands
and breathed softly into your mouth:
Hi baby, how are you?
And carefully, so carefully,
whispered *Tonight?* As if to promise
both of us that the baby would sleep,
the dog would stop barking,
the woman,
outside,
shrieking to her man, would find solace.
Then, putting our phones on silent,
so, I could fall into you, as greedy and
reckless as that very first time.

Black, Black, Black

Late Spring. My lover's hair holds the heat
and light of the afternoon sun, which
falls through the trees in leaf-shaped pieces.
I wrap my hand in and around the thick strands
brushing against her shoulders.
Pulling her head back, taut, I nip
a small red kiss in the cream of her neck.
Let her go. Against the lids of my shuttered eyes
light spangles and refracts,
small pops of gold and silver.

We are our lazy, weekend selves,
bodies soft and open. I stretch,
luxuriously, on the rough picnic blanket,
grasp a bottle of water from the esky
and tip it back, slowly,
and swallow. Our daughter mashes berries
in her plump fists, and the jewelled black
of insects march purposefully,
head to tail,
head to tail,
in rhythmic lines
towards our spent crumbs.

The Two Fridas

Eight Weeks

For Julia

You were only a small amalgam of cells,
and as they divided and grew
into body parts, arm and leg buds, the tiny curved,
tail that would become your spine,
something went awry.
I wish there was a better way to describe it.
But I lost it all. I felt as you left me,
the presence of pain, sharp as a sickle,
pressing on my belly from the inside out,
followed by a swift, unwelcome wash of copper,
where blood should not have been.

I lost it all: your anniversaries, birthdays.
First birthday cake smash,
second birthday slide and ball pit,
third birthday running around with your friends from day care.
That *Frozen* cake with the moulded Anna and Elsa.
Then walking you home from school, white socks grey with dirt
at the end of the day, scuffed Mary Janes, or sneakers,
your pigtail loose at the nape of your neck,
or short hair lifting in the breeze.
Or asleep; at six or ten years old,
your sweaty curls mashed into the pillow,
your favourite book tucked under one arm.
It felt as if your leaving was
inconsequential to everyone but your father
and me.
Both of us inconsolable and incomplete.

The Second
For Verity

Only half born and she was already crying,
with her head breaching my vulva,
just after the crisp snick
of the episiotomy into my perineum,
before the doctor could rotate
her left shoulder and
deliver her body into his hands,
and the only time during a labour I was
given a mirror, I watched her—born.
Entranced at the sight of her head in the speckled glass,
my fingertips against her wrinkled scalp,
wet and fuzzy and warm
as it appeared and disappeared,
between contractions.

Then wholly delivered, red-faced and furious.
Afterwards I sat, cross-legged, on the delivery table,
stitched up, high on endorphins,
nursing her in my arms, as her anemone
mouth turned and opened, not to suckle my nipple, but
two of the fingers on her right hand.

She, then only two hours old,
Already utterly herself.

In the Beginning

How could it be ten months
since they pulled you, quiet and rheumy-eyed
from your mother's body?
Since your skull
was knit with electrodes, endless slashes
and beeps on a greyscale screen?

So many duskies.

I almost—almost—got used
to the midwives swooping in,
clicking their tongues in dismay,
cooing your name,
rubbing your face and feet
to make you breathe again.

Two days old before you cried
and even then, you punched
above your weight, with a small, fierce sound
I recognised each time I entered the nursery.
You shared the space with babies
as small as kittens, tucked safely in plastic boxes,
attached to all manner of wiring,
information on monitors
I read like an expert:
temperature, oxygen sats, heart rate, blood pressure.

All those weeks we worried and waited,
travelling to the hospital while it was still purple dawn

spending fifteen hours a day by your side.
Our lips cracked and eyes gritty
from the steady heat in the nursery.
Our goal: a 40 ml feed, before we could take you home,
but you could only manage an exhausted suckle of 25 ml,
and then the nasogastric tube for the rest.

But this morning I watched you twirl
your bottle in your hands like a cheerleader's baton,
guzzle 200 ml and fling the bottle aside as you
squirmed free of my arms, to launch
yourself onto your next adventure.

Late

For Olive

You drum your feet on the floor,
arch your back,
scream and push at me, a tattoo of feet
against my chest,
bite your fist, then
sink your teeth into the back of my hand,
leaving behind a perfect crescent of indentations.

Late to language,
you were so frustrated.
We tried hard to guess.
Do you want a hug?
No!
Water?
No!
Milk?
No, you say, *no,*
but you reach for the bottle, regardless.
You have,
I have counted,
precisely
52 words.

Little Bird

I check my phone with bleary eyes,
It's 5.30 am. I call out to the baby
—who has climbed down from the bed,
and is fossicking among my things—
to please come back to sleep.
She ignores me, destroying the careful
arrangement of objects on my bedside table.
She, all ready to start her day, with or without me.
Shaking and preening her feathers,
casting her warble to the early morning sky.
Come back to bed, honey, I say. *Please.*
As if words could harness the wind.

To Shrink Until I Am Small
For Nicky and Nathan

I want to travel far with you.
I want this and love this:
the sun hot on my shoulders
and the careful weight
of all our belongings on my back.
I collect stones the size of wrist bones
hide them in my pockets for hundreds of days,
all of them worn smooth,
the colours of the ocean where we found them.
Sometimes when you do not notice
I take a picture of you and this moment,
captured now, and forever. Something to share.
Something planted, something
borrowed, something new.

Inheritance

For Javier

You rang me late last night. I was up, writing.
You said,
I want you to see some poems I have written.
I wait for my Gmail to load,
your breath a wash of sound in my ear.
Finally, before me, a sonnet, a haiku
and a free-verse poem, with lines
of iambic pentameter I counted off on my fingers.

And while it is years since I sang and read to you,
teaching you the rhythms and joys of language,
within you, I see, I run, humming. I have
bequeathed to you an ambiguous heritage,
the dual legacies of melancholy and insomnia,
both of us up late, not sleeping, both of us writing,
but, like the fairy's parting gift to Sleeping Beauty,
there is a salve to soothe your mind's sharp sting.
An ability to wrestle flesh and feeling from words.

A River in Your Hands

For Nicky and Olive

Every night you say goodnight
to a growing list of things:
blowing kisses to your Elsa doll.
Waving grandly to your constant
companion, the monkey,
with whom you sleep
and play and who you
carry to the park.

Earlier, on the kitchen bench, you showed
such ebullience for a dinner of
scrambled eggs and cheese,
followed by $7 blackberries
from your grandmother,
as you beamed sweetly purple
on your chin and nose and
demanded *More, Mama, please.*

At Hyde Park with your sister,
it's to the ibis pecking for insects,
the ducks you chase, the errant crows,
even women strangers passing by.

You bestow your heart
a dozen times a day, at least, to
the Thermomix,
the bottle-maker,
the microwave.

This evening it was to your toothbrush,
Hi brush, bye brush, love you brush,
wriggling your bottom on the vanity,
your feet flexing like baby starfish
in the basin, as you scrubbed
your tongue clean and licked toothpaste
like honey from your fingers.

Blue Wren

Think of a bird,
think of how it died,
its small-boned self, smashed
against your kitchen window.
One solitary deep blue feather,
a tiny smear of blood and flesh
that you will clean later with newspaper and ammonia.

Think of a bird's frail body sinking into hollow bones,
still but for the breeze that stirs its thinning feathers.
Think of teams of ants, think of flies
laying maggots into the small cave of a belly,
picked clean by scavengers.

Think of your child finding this bird,
a scrap of faded blue at her feet. She looks up at you,
expecting, like last time, a shoebox and a cloth.

Some kind of ritual.

Flowers from the garden.
A cross made out of popsticks.

Some words spoken.

But it is late in the afternoon,
she needs a bath and pyjamas
and something to eat before bed.
And you are tired.

Tired of how they come at you,
their small dark bodies falling, straight as arrows
from the sky, almost one a week,
to smash their fragile skulls against
your deadly, transparent panes of glass.

Self-Portrait with Thorn Necklace and Hummingbird

At Four

He's in the bath.
I'm in the bathroom.
This is how it starts.

At Seven

At seven I had a doll's house. Not the one I wanted,
which had flights of stairs, lamps that switched on and off,
old-fashioned furniture, and teeny-tiny cups and saucers,
but a flat-roofed, grey plywood, single-storey box.
Its windows and doors were empty rectangles
cut into the wood, front and back,
with two rooms on either side of a wallpapered corridor.

At seven I made furniture out of LEGO
beds and chairs from red and yellow bricks.
At seven I fashioned curtains out of tissues and sticky tape.
Decorated them with Texta dots. I left
crumbs from my sandwiches for the fairies
who visited when I was asleep.

At seven he was the monster that hid beneath my bed.
The scratching of branches late at night against my window.
The strong arm of our family's law.

At seven I had a red, plastic torch and I read
beneath the covers until the batteries went flat,
my little halo of safety, that shiny light of moon against the blanket,
until there was a tap upon my head.

At seven he was the secret I had learnt to keep.

At seven I read all the books my mother bought instead of lollies.
Enid Blyton was my favourite author
and I wrote her countless letters,
asking if I could be in one of her adventures.

Of course she never answered.

At Eight

I was eight years old the first time it happened:
growing a row of ulcers
between my teeth and bottom lip.
A jangle of heat and cold
as if a nerve had been exposed.

A rough topography inside my mouth,
each sore a millimetre or two wide.
Wafers of skin repeatedly
worried at by the tip of my tongue.
My mother bought me SM-33 from the chemist.
Sullen brown, it stung,
and tasted bittersweet and medicinal.

Actions that should have been rudimental
jolted me out of comfort, each mouthful of food
a labour to chew and swallow, each word
I spoke softly frayed at the edges.

I felt dirty, somehow; ill-used.
The doctor said my system was inflamed
and ordered blood tests and took swabs.

I also had my grandmother's trick:
piercing a Vitamin E capsule with a safety pin,
then anointing each ulcer with its honey-coloured fluid.

My flesh, in five days' time,
was whole again, intact:
the very definition
of integrity.

At Nine

It's autumn in my backyard.
The dry, brown leaves, big as saucers,
crunch beneath my feet as I walk through them
up to my ankles. With my dirt-stained hands
I water the leaves with a dribbly hose,
pretending they're cornflakes and the hose is milk,
singing, under my breath,
all the songs I know from *The Sound of Music*.
Then I make up advertisements
for hair shampoo and breakfast cereal.
My left hand as a microphone.
Curtseying as gracefully as I can
before my invisible audience.
Before my invisible friends.

At Thirteen

Not that I was beautiful,
but I was alive
and voracious,
bleeding
so prettily,
red roses on a white cotton pad.
I rang my mother to say *it's here, it's here,*
she, who had bled at ten, she who had
stockpiled pads for me
in the bathroom
since my ninth year,
waiting so impatiently for me to grow up.
I know she rang my father.
Did they celebrate like I did?
Finally, in a body that fit.

At Sixteen

Well, does he then?
my father demands. *Fuck you?* His voice,
like rocks thrown at a stained-glass window.
I quietly shatter
—at his language,
but not the question.
There are so few secrets here.

As I search for my sneakers under the bed,
he pulls me up roughly by my shoulder, shakes me,
repeatedly, as if I'm a dog.
I asked you a question, Miss.
And I want to tell him the truth. *No.*
I am too scared; the boy is too shy.
But, instead,
I look him straight in the eyes,
brave for once,

and lie.

At Seventeen

There was a truth some girls had to learn (so Janis sang)
that love was only for beauty queens
—and I was not close to being one of those.
In love with words and unsuitable people,
searching for someone who would
scour my heavy flesh, fill the hole
in the centre of my chest.
Like a child who still believed in fairytales,
I longed to be plucked from my family
and placed into another life. Instead,
I fell in love with other people's parents,
befriended other people's siblings.
Only seventeen, I would lie in bed, curled in on myself,
writing poems on scraps of paper
I would later burn to ash.

At Twenty

For Claire

I gave birth to you
with the admonitions of the doctor and midwives, to
Push, into your bottom, that's the girl.
I had no idea what I was doing,
the numbness of the epidural overtaking instinct.
As I pushed into my face so hard
I popped blood vessels in my eyes and cheeks,
then vomited my lunch into a grey plastic bowl
moments before you were born.

On the third day, as you were wheeled
by your father, all the way from the nursery
to my inexpert arms, I stood in front of the bathroom mirror
and sobbed (they said it was the baby blues).
I had rock-hard, leaking breasts,
a soggy stomach and plum-black bruises
from my belly to my thighs.

You had a white suck blister on your upper lip
and the palest blush of crimson on one cheek from the forceps
used to gouge you out of my unwilling body.
Your father would put his smallest finger in your mouth
and marvel at the strength of your suckle.

And while I marvelled at your commonplace things: fingers, toes,
mouth, and nose, it was your tiny fist kneading my breast,
your dark eyes reflecting the 2.00 am news that won me over.

At Twenty-four

I did not even know how much I wanted
a son until he was born.
Girls were easy, and I had two of them,
as a girl myself, but he would make me an adult.
No more ringing my mother for advice
at the slightest sign of a fever or a sniffle.
Down's syndrome, they said. *Heart defects.*

All I wanted to do was take him home
and rock him, safe.
I would show them all, I thought, as I
whispered impossible things in his ear,
a life spread out like a map before us,
with mazes and cul-de-sacs
where a child could play in safety.

This would be our story.

But one December morning
his heart exploded in his chest
and not even the best doctor in the country
could piece it back together.

They showed me his body, lying
in the middle of a hospital bed, with the rails turned down.
I went to tell them he would fall, it was dangerous,
How could they be so careless?
But I caught myself just in time.
All I remember doing after that was cupping my hands

around my eyes, pressing my face against the window,
surveying the grass and road below
with forensic precision. Carefully licking
the glass my nose was pressed against,
dust and grit on my tongue, acrid and bitter.
Grains of sand and fine dust coating my mouth.

Much later I learnt from mythology that
this is how clay becomes flesh:
dust and grit mixed with saliva,
A creature brought forth from pulverised stone.

At Twenty-eight

I was pregnant for the seventh time,
fat as a seal, listing south,
anaemic, with a pale, dry mouth
and an endless thirst for iceblocks.
I remember standing in the shower, legs outspread,
so tired sometimes that I would slide
carefully, pendulously, down the wet, tiled wall
and let the water beat on my head like a drum.
Social Services allocated me a cleaner,
and I would get up early before she came, and make the beds,
feed breakfast to the younger children, settle the kitchen to
rights,
and send the older ones to school. My belly,
the veins in my legs and vulva, hung
like ripe bunches of grapes,
pounding with all that extra blood, as I smoothed
the sleek brown head of that child, or this,
gathering them to myself and waiting.

At Thirty-three

I had to laugh when you told me
I was the same age as Jesus,
when he was crucified.
And what have you done? you asked.
Headed up any major religions?
I am at university, being acknowledged
for my brain, instead of my uterus.
Three units of psychology, and one of creative writing.
I am getting HDs and coming home at 6.30 pm
to a houseful of rowdy children,
wanting a little of my time.
Five daughters,
and the three youngest have headlice.
They take turns sitting in front of me,
and I harvest their hair with a fine-tooth comb,
multi-tasking, asking them about their day,
listening to their reading while I'm
crunching the fat carapaces of the lice
between my fingernails and onto a tissue.
Then getting all the children into bed,
and studying from midnight until 3.00 am
when everyone, including my husband, is asleep.
No, I say, *no major religion.*

At Thirty-eight

In the middle of trying to tell you
that this time I think I'm going under,
we are interrupted by the mournful wailing of the fire trucks outside,
and then the angry crackle and snap of the fire.

We run outside, the kids streaming behind us,
as the fire trucks *chug chug*, stationary on the road,
as the static of the walkie-talkies, and
the hiss of water from the hoses interrupts
my swift counting of the children.

I start again,
my eyes flicking over each head,
but in the middle of counting—
chunks of our remembered conversation
float to the surface of my consciousness
your angry words, my vain attempts to explain to you
what is happening—
seem wrong, somehow in this summer season
where everything teams with life.

The fire scribbles the sky with smoke,
the sun, pendulous and simmering, as
I shade my eyes, call out to the kids, who are
running excitedly backwards and forwards from the verge
with all the other kids on our street, *to come back here, now,* as

they call to me *Mama, can you see the fire? Can you?*

I think of the potential for tragedy,
so close in this summer of fire and conversations.
We both bear witness to it.
The proximity of devastation catching in our throats.

At Forty

I drank from a De Bortoli's four-litre cask,
poured into the large, light blue bell of my glass.
At least three a night, a bottle's worth,
making the children my accomplices,
then vodka from the freezer, in orange juice,
so strong it made my lips numb.

I didn't fool anyone, not even myself, as
I painstakingly kissed their foreheads
with my liquor-stained mouth.
I had three chemists on rotation for my pills,
fretting when my supply of them was low.

From a distance I would listen, aghast, at the lies
I told, the worlds I destroyed,
as I hurled myself heedlessly through all our lives.

At Forty-five

I hurt myself today
with the metal pin of a green glass brooch
I keep hidden in my toiletry bag.
Four searches of my belongings
and they are yet to find it.
My doctor says I will be discharged if I don't stop.
That's no incentive.

The setting is Modern-slash-Danish,
pale wood, picture windows,
and fresh flowers at the nurses' station.
This is private insurance mental health care:
middle-aged women with earbuds
and interesting jewellery,
high-achieving teenagers,
gaunt and fractious,
roaming the halls.

And in all of this, moments of clarity in sharp relief:
the gouged marks of the metal pin, on my arms.
My black jumper stiff with blood.

At Fifty-two
A response to 'The Recluse' by Randolph Stow

I: Then
Riding the train

10.30 am: I should be at work.
10.30 am: The woman's mellow voice comes over the
loudspeaker.

On my own aboard this monstrous metal engine,
so many times I have taken this journey.
I watch as kilometres of anonymous sky fly by.
I buy, time after time: an all-day ticket.
No-one knows me here. No-one cares. I am
an automatic insatiable engine, counting down the minutes,

10.40 am.
10.50 am.

Stop. Start again. Stop, the hours of travel
broken up into five- and ten-minute intervals.

II
I have the diagnosis: menorrhagia:
a hot spatter, almost always unexpected,
a crimson stain spreading onto my white skirt,
or onto my dress. Blood-soaked knickers
at any time of the month.
I have the diagnosis: incontinence: shitting myself
because I can't make it to the toilet in time—a triptych of
PTSD, Irritable Bowel, and a loose sphincter
from too many kids, my doctor says.

III

I am wet and sticky. I smell like shit.
I try in vain to wipe myself clean
with handfuls of toilet wipes, then
scrub my belly and thighs
with water and stiff paper towel
from the dispenser, hiding, half-naked
in the stinking metal toilet stall
at whichever station I pressed the bell for.
I wrestle clean underwear
and flannels from plastic ziplock bags
I keep in my handbag.

IV

Back on the train I close my eyes to the click and shutter
of these chattering strips of light,
a recluse on this anonymous afternoon's journey.
I've been here so often I've learnt all the stations off by heart:
Welshpool–Queen's Park–Cannington;
Challis–Sherwood–Armadale,
the *clackety clack* of metal on metal the only noise that soothes me,
this carriage the only place that demands nothing of me, but time.
My head bumps rhythmically against the window,
my cheek invisibly chalked with the skin cells
of a thousand previous faces.

V

My mind is a revolving line of unspooling track, pebbles for words,
going forward and back, forward and back, my teeth lightly chatter
in this hermetically sealed, air-conditioned tube.
Slicing through my invisible wounds like light through glass.

I have to get off the train again, my body barely
holding back the flood of diarrhoea, cramping, sweat dripping,
my body bends and sways as the train stops.

Pulling my bag onto my shoulder,
my feet firmly planted,
hurrying, hurrying away.

VI

Despite all the preparation, despite
the specialists' visits and myriad procedures,
despite handfuls of different coloured pills,
swallowed with water that is blood-warm
and tastes like the metal
of this stall, it is here I have ended up,
scrubbing underwear in a restroom sink
until my knuckles are raw,
washing shit or blood clots down the plughole.

VII: Now
Landscape

My landscape is an overworn garment, my body is
pressed and repressed, darts let out,
seams undone. Everything soft and loose,
with all my days collected and broken up, stacked like driftwood,
the passing decades riven and fragmented.

All my days picked at and scrutinised,
and at my back I always hear time's winged chariot,
(as co-passenger and confidante), hurrying near.
Alas, I think, alas, the years slip by; with so little notice taken.

Costa Branca, I am blood and shit and water,
my body a mass of softened hills, as white as wool,
intercut with tattooed pathways,
tears streaming down my face like the hard, bright sea.
There, in that carriage, was my memory.

At Fifty-four

Here I am, aged fifty-four, with a pregnant wife.
Ten years we have planned for this.
We have a baby name book, which is hopefully inscribed

with our names and the date from back then—2007—
and piles of books and clothes bought in anticipation of you.
The odds were stacked against you, with only a 30% chance

of getting through the first trimester, and, thereafter,
fortnightly appointments, bloods, and scans.
I lie in bed, while your mother sleeps, my head

against her shoulder and wrap my arm around her belly.
You kick hard against my hand, as if to
promise me: I am here; I will be with you soon.

I have to hold you to that. Hold onto the thought of you,
pressing your head against the neck of her ripening womb.
It feels like a promise fulfilled when you are finally born,

my faith in you has been repaid. From the very beginning
you have so many faces: awake, asleep, in repose, eyes alight,
white teeth gleaming in a pink mouth; you have defied us all.

At Fifty-six

I am covered in tattoos, my favourite fabric.
And as I lift my two arms high above my head,
the shirt I am wearing falls away
from my wrists to my shoulders
and everyone can see, covering my arms
the rainbow of colour I love so much.

In private I hold the skin and the soft, pale fat
of my inner thigh between my two hands.
S t r e t c h it until it goes taut
and then let it go. It settles in place.
I imagine the pieces of art that could be possible
if only I had different legs,
smooth, tanned, and muscled,
two lithe new canvases to be filled.

I think of this body: round belly—no good—and back,
at a pinch, still an available site to colour.
Hands and neck, all forbidden spaces
for a middle-aged woman.
I think about the ownership of this body:
and how I have been able to choose this skin I wear.

The Broken Column

Petrichor: November 7, 2020

A response to 'Simplicities of Summer' by Randolph Stow

We are living in a time of unseasonal rain.
Allegheny, Atlanta, Clark County.
Strange names that have grown
familiar with days of repetition.
Talking heads continue to count the election results,
we exhale as one, as the numbers stack up,
slowly, in our favour.

At 4.00 am
I leave the television to
the darkness of the room, the fading red
and growing swathe of blue states
on large computer screens,
the broadly arched American accents,
interchangeable faces on every channel.

I can hear the soft summer rain against the windows,
I have been watching the TV for hours. Stiff, bone weary.
Chip packets, cheese rinds, and popcorn
litter the coffee table. A bottle and the red dregs of two wine glasses.
I unlock the front door and go outside.
My lungs flex and stretch,
I open my mouth
stick out my tongue,
pink and fluted as a deep-sea creature.
It unfurls, gently
rests on my bottom lip.
The fall of water sizzles and pops,

shattering on my warm flesh
like longed for rain on hungry earth.
My upturned mouth,
full at last
and deliciously wet.

The Boys Who Dream of Winter
For Danny and Matthew

I

His biggest problem until then was how to flow on the field
like slow electricity, sinew and bone, ribbons of breath
drawn in and let out like a birthday whistle, then held;
all volatility of motion and emotion, flawless in execution.
The *oohs* and *aahs* of the home crowd that night
like any other—the most bitter regret of
his parents, they did not call to ask *How was the game?*

There was no lick of warning at the edges of sight,
no prickle of caution: *Here comes trouble, Danny Boy. Run.*
It was, they said *a coward's punch*—
the singular collision of flesh and concrete.

His mother sits beside him now, his capable, square-tipped hand
pliant as a child's in hers. She breathes in disinfectant and elastoplast
and the familiar sour-sweet tang of the little boy
from those easy, early days; a rising star with Ronaldo plastered on his wall.

She documents each freckle and each smudge of skin, counting slowly
up from zero, the passing sweep of the second hand
punctuating each passing hour, each night, each day,
each measured, staccato hiss of the machine, his lungs
inflating and deflating.
What else is there to do but trace with her eyes all the tubes,
blood, and urine lines disappearing and reappearing and
the tracery of veins on the skin of his inner arm—
and start her counting again?

II

Twenty years ago:
The moon shone coldly, turning to black
the blood on his face, a clown's leered mouth and eyes
on skin as frail as rice paper. The moon slipped in and out
of clouds, hiding and seeking:
he was unrecognisable as human in the half-light.
When they first saw him, they thought he was
some farmer's punchline: a cap, a bundle of torn clothes,
lolling head of straw strung up and pistol-whipped
on the boundary fence. The susurration of each laboured breath,
his 100-pound doll's body all bones,
plinking like a xylophone in the breeze.

She was spared this first sight of him,
the gauzy swathe of mosquitos humming around his head,
grass and mud churned up on the ground beneath him,
tyre tracks, boot prints, his arms and legs trussed
with wire, all bony feet and elbows,
sacrificed on the altar of bigotry.

He became, like every victim taken too early,
a life reduced to headlines,
A moniker to be recalled on each anniversary. *Remembering
Matthew*, the banner title reads—five, ten, fifteen years on,
the accompanying photograph,
all soft mouth, and the sharp cut of cheekbones smeared
and pixilated, buried on the inner pages.
On the evening news he is a cautionary tale, history
for young boys everywhere, and for a mother who mourns.

Tutankhamun's Box

Almost disregarded by those
twentieth-century men in frockcoats, stomping
through tombs, searching only for obvious wealth:
gold and lapis lazuli—The Big Find,
disinterested in what lay at the Boy King's feet. Inside
a box within a box, inlaid plaster on wood,
depicting Osiris, God of the Dead,
they found preserved: skin like parchment, stretched taut
over bird-like bones and thinly fuzzing hair.

Two stillborn girls.

Those early scientists were quick to diagnose
all that was wrong with them:
spina bifida,
scoliosis,
a dislodged and broken scapula. But these
post-mortem injuries slandered
the consanguineous union of Tut and his younger sister.

Compare the broken bones of modernity to the care of those
who had preserved the babes' integrity.
Twin sisters preserved for millennia
in precious salt and embalming resins, wrapped in
strips of linen inlaid with herbs—little chicks
whose mouths would have sung of family, and
their two young parents, painfully bereaved,
their accumulation of grief moving through the centuries
like marsh grasses swaying in the breeze.

Two silent birds.

The Blue Nile itself, silty and pregnant
with promise,
spilling open every season of plenty.

In the Country

That first day at a new school, moving thirty miles
inland, from Albany to Mount Barker. A different world.
Country kids in jeans and check shirts,
and more swearing in that first recess than I'd heard in my life.
I wore my red corduroy pants suit
and brown suede shoes with the stacked heels,
the height of fashion in Albany, in 1976.

The girls at the back of the class laughed at me
in plain sight of the teacher, mimicking my soft voice and accent.
She ignored them and asked the girl in the second row,
with her caterpillar eyebrows and her brown hair in pigtails, to be
my friend. She stuck with me valiantly, for a day or two,
and then followed her friends
as they ran away from me, squealing with laughter. I only
ran after them once, on the third day. Unable to catch them,
I then asked the teacher if I could stay in at recess,
clean the blackboards and beat chalk dust from the dusters.

Those same kids later took pity on me,
cornered me in the playground
and taught me how to sit as they did, *Like this, stupid, sit like a boy*,
as my legs obediently splayed, hands spread wide on my thighs,
in jeans bought from the Co-op on the corner of Lowood Road.
I learnt to say *Fuck off, dickhead* to the boy who liked me,
to the boy I also liked, my pang of regret every time
he turned an ugly red looking in my direction,
our casual cruelty as we ran from him, laughing,
four girls together, leaving him alone
to the jeers and teasing of his mates.

Sisters

A circle of light quivering onto the roof of my bedroom
from the metal night-light,
we lay on the floor, hip to hip, your hands cupped expectantly
against your chin. And as I gathered these stories together
like beads from the floor, north and south, west and east,
rolling them in my palm like quicksilver,
stitching a life together from stiff sheets of paper
and different coloured inks, I read you *The Muddle-Headed Wombat*.
Rolling the voices in my throat, round or squeaky, or ponderous,
as you tilted your head blissfully against my shoulder,
refusing to look outside the light to the darkness beyond,
trying to be brave, the two of us.

Fourth Avenue

I'd trade most of it, to have you back again, Granny,
to have your short, full body pressed closely against mine,
comforting and warm in your blue cotton skirt and white blouse,
your apron tied around your waist,
as we walked together towards the corner.
Your strong, lined hand enveloped mine, your nervous
thumb pressing and pressing against the skin on the back of my hand as we
walked down Fourth Avenue, to visit our neighbours.

I always had to play with their daughter, who everyone called
slow, and I didn't really understand what that meant,
but it had something to do with her having the best toys,
and me being eight years old and jealous.
I still recall the day that I, covetous and canny,
forced her to change bikes with me, her giant fourteen-year-old limbs
pedalling awkwardly on my tiny trike and me, pedalling to
freedom on her snazzy two-wheeler,
with its pink trim and silver training wheels.

I was scared of her father, who smelled like bitter Emu Export,
Huge, wet half-moons in his armpits,
every day, stacking brown longnecks in formation
against the outside bin, always shouting at the commentators on the footy,
and at everyone in the room, especially my grandfather.
Even though they both barracked for the same team.

Her mother stayed in the kitchen, gossiping with you.
I had recently learnt that adults ignored me
if I read or played with toys

as if in a world of my own.
I would take three or four seconds
to lift my head and answer if I was spoken to.
I knew when something particularly juicy came up,
because you'd both suddenly take notice of me
and I'd get told to *Go away and check on Linda,*
and I would, for the shortest time possible,
until I slowly crept back,
to hear the latest gossip about our neighbours,
and their kids, both of you looking at me and away,
carved in statue likenesses of guilty children.

Ambitions

My parents' plans for me,
dizzying in their simplicity:
be the first in my family to attend university.
Be a teacher or a librarian.
Work hard,
pass,
get a job.
The soft bigotry of their low expectations—
surpassed.

The Secret Sea

Even talking about it.

Stop.

Even talking about it.

Stop.

Brings me to my knees.
I have returned my children to the briny sea from where they once came.

Rocks shaped like fists bruise my toes,
cut the soles of my feet
until my blood seeps into the water,
crimson mingling to pink, like chrysanthemums
floating at the ragged edges of this secret sea.

The stars creep across the sky slowly,
as if in an opium haze, I lean out
and catch them before they fall.

I am a woman, bereft.
I walk further into the water,
the sand suckles at my feet and shins with the toothless gums of babies.

I hear the wailing, now.
Closer and closer.
Our voices sliding through the seagrasses
and out beyond the break of rocks, to join the water
that foams and belches in the salt-laden air.

In Which a Universe Resides

I imagine its PacMan mouths devouring her healthy flesh,
chomping on her spine and brain
where metastases bloom like evil fruit.
There is nothing metaphorical about it.
Her flesh and bone are being consumed.
Her blood carries its tracer cells
to spots in her head and pelvis

like spores on the breeze, or like sentinels,
at the farthest flung outposts of her body,
to set up camp. Then darkness overwhelmed the earth,
which is to say last week she went blind for an hour,
something in her brain pressing on her optic nerve,
then, like stuttered electricity, repeated seizures.
Five, at first, then nine. Today, eleven.

My son-in-law tells me about a book he just read,
I think it was titled *We Contain Multitudes*,
which perfectly suits this analogy: he says that
in every body there is a universe of sorts,
heat and entropy, composition, and decomposition,
which says as much as anything could
about what we are expecting.

So Beautiful

At six you told me I looked like my father.
Even then, I understood your disappointment.
You were so small boned that at ten I could not get
your wedding ring past the first joint of my finger.
Like an ugly stepsister, I could not squeeze into your shoes.
The family joked about my Welsh hands and feet.

A model in your teens and twenties,
with your wide mouth and almond eyes
did you believe your only worth was in
how you looked? I'm afraid
you may never have seen yourself
as anything more than surface deep,
 as anything more than a painted face.

I grew sick of trying to measure up.
Of trying and failing.
Trying and failing.
On the cracked-ice surface of things,
simultaneously not being enough,
and being entirely too much to bear.

Crows on a Road Trip to Mount Barker

While we hurtle past them at 110 km/h,
they *hop hop* to safety at the very last moment, as if
double daring us to avoid them, their heads
jutting like priests on their way to Mass,
proud-breasted, frocked in glossy black feathers.
Apparently, they have excellent memories,
and an elaborate social system of manners and mores.
But here on the road they are simply what nature intended:
rubbish collectors, picking each carcass clean to white bone.

Plague animals—snakes and frogs—rustle in the undergrowth.

We are surrounded by all these man-made things:
sheep trucks thundering past us on their way to slaughter,
blue-painted tree trunks, memorials to young men's suicides,
the counted white crosses adorning the side of the road,
mute witnesses to fatigue and inattention, adorned with
rings of plastic flowers and gaudy sateen ribbons.

As we sit in the safe bubble of our vehicle
the hungry crows gorge themselves on roadkill:
a roo or a fox pulped to its constitutive parts
—pelt and flesh smeared like meat paste on the road.

This Way Clad

Clad only in air,
dripping water onto the mat,
wet and exposed
in the harsh bathroom light.
I stare vacantly into the mirror, wipe it clean of fog.
Before me, my pendulous stomach,
hanging parcels of breasts,
nipples pointing downwards
lax chin, and soft arms.

Wherever I go,
imprinted on each ribbon of DNA,

I carry my father with me.

Fishing with My Father, 1974

That Sunday afternoon,
the two of us, fishing from the rocks.
Standing just clear of the black moss
at the water's edge, the grey striations of a fish
flopping in my hand, as I tore the hook
from its mouth, under his direction:
Gentle, gentle. No need to tear it.
Under the matching grey of an Albany sky,
I hunched against the wind in my jeans, and
fishing jumper, stiff on the front
with fish guts and whale oil.
I flung my burley and whale-oil mix
as far as I could into the water,
a prismatic slick like petrol, mirrored by
the sleek bellies of the skippy in the bucket.

As he took his serrated knife, and twisted his hand,
spearing the fish I'd just caught through its eye,
he told me about a friend of his,
with more money than sense,
who fished in cashmere sweaters.
My father clucked his tongue,
scrubbed his hands together,
and stood up, tall compared to me, saying:
They were all the colours of the rainbow, Bron.

Circling

Over the clatter of plates
and the anonymity of a local café,
you give me a signet ring of Granny's,
which you confess was always meant for me
and which you've kept safely for years.
I will lose it from my finger in less than a week.

I have a confession of my own:
I tell you about our father,
not expecting you to believe me,
but you do.

Upon hearing my words
amidst the clamour,
you are silent,
playing the images I speak of on repeat,
as sharks circle in your head,
their black fins cutting shapes in
the churning water.

A Letter to My Mother

Do you remember how my father kept his old razor blades
on the bedhead in your bedroom? And how my sister,
aged three, found them, sliced her fingers to ribbons
and you beat her for not knowing better than to touch your things?

Or how you locked me, five years old, in my room,
while you and my father had lazy, Sunday morning sex, and
I pissed all over the floor, as I tried in vain to reach
the doorknob to get out? How infuriating I was to you, not beautiful,

but the image of him and his mother. Do you know years later
when I found a picture of myself, aged nine, I ached
for that earnest little girl in the green Martian costume,
already battle-hardened, with her knock knees and crooked mouth.

You would go days and days without speaking to me,
bestowing your words like bounty on everyone else in the family.
We were mere body heat, passing in the hallway without touching, until
the silence stretched taut as wire and I would do *anything* for words.

Metastases

So many things are broken,
the ring you gave me has lost a stone,
my stained-glass bowl has a smashed stem
from when the baby threw it in anger.
But the heart is not a dish or a cup,
that slips from clumsy fingers.

It sits in its cage, precisely beats
with blood, and were it cut adrift
from its muscular wall to hang
in the stinging air
would continue to
sing,
sing,
to its irrevocable end.

Augury

For Saebah

A response to 'Amaryllis Belladonna' by Randolph Stow.

Sometimes I waken to the unexpected slap of sunrise,
or to a season stripped to the bone,
where sepia gusts rattle the window sashes.
It is the reminder of yesterday afternoon that makes me stir,

when the sky was heavy with crows,
which I couldn't help but see as a portent of some kind, even
though they simply heralded the coming storm.
Their mournful cawing to one another
stopped my conversation, and it was, instead,
you I thought of, soft, and pale and swollen,
with the purple smear of fatigue under your eyes, and your
voice thin and reedy in my ear.

Our daily phone call.

The things that grow
inside you are strange
and I do not understand them—
is that a terrible thing to say?
Waving in your body's darkness
and moving in surges with the pulsing of your blood.
And as I waited for the world to stop,
the crows arced across the sky as one,
their wings beating in balletic motion,
chests straining with the effort to hold their form,
as they threatened to bring the kicking and clawing
night into the room with me
to settle in cold drifts at my feet.

Letters and Love Songs

I remember:
one evening when he snuck me out of bed,
and took both of us into the lounge room
to watch *Macbeth* on the television.
Have I told you that I burst with joy?

Although I mostly recall
his hands, as strong, swift to punish, with a closed fist
to my belly, or a careless backhand
that stained my cheek,

while the witches
chanted their incantations, on the black and white screen,
those same hands
gently carded the soft wings of my hair.
And it was safe to sleep.

Acknowledgements

Some of these poems have appeared in earlier iterations and in other publications. 'Orange Madonna,' 'Sunday Evening, 9.42 pm,' and 'To Shrink Until I Am Small' appeared in *Poetry d'Amour* in 2019. 'To You' appeared in *Poetry d'Amour* in 2020. 'The Girl of My Eyes' appeared in *Poetry d'Amour* 2021. 'Blue Wren,' 'Fishing with My Father, 1974,' appeared in *Bent Street* 4.2. 'Augury,' 'Kintsugi,' 'At Fifty-Two' and 'Petrichor: November 7, 2020' (all responses to poems by Randolph Stow), appeared in *Westerly Magazine,* issue 66.1. 'At Twenty-eight' appeared in *What We Carry: An Anthology of Childbearing* (Recent Work Press, 2021). 'At Twenty-four' appeared in *Grieve* 2021. I read the poems 'Remembrance of an Open Wound' and 'The Wounded Deer' online from *What the Water Gave Me: Poems After Frida Kahlo* by Pascale Petit (Seren Books, 2010). 'The Two Fridas' line, 'a skein of memory the connection of future and past,' adapted from lines in the poem 'A Body Inside' by Michelle Cahill in *What We Carry*. 'At Seventeen' references the song of the same name by Janis Ian (*Between the Lines*, Columbia, 1975). At Twenty-four' lines about dirt adapted from the poem 'Pica' by Jennifer Perrine. 'Metastases' ideas for lines about the heart from the poem 'Proposition' by Liana Joy Christensen in *Letters to Our Home: Creative Reflections on the Climate Crisis*, (Mulla Mulla Press, 2020).

I acknowledge the Whadjuk people of the Noongar nation as the traditional owners and custodians of the land on which I work. I offer my respects to Whadjuk Elders past, present and emerging. Always was, always will be, Aboriginal land.

I have a number of people to thank for their help in putting this collection together. Firstly, my profound thanks to my editor Georgia Richter who has the uncanny knack of revealing a poem's true dimensions and her many hours of work is the reason that so many of these poems hang together as they do. It is always a pleasure to work with Georgia. My special thanks must also go to Claire Miller and Chloe Walton for their wise counsel and generosity. It is a pleasure to again be with Fremantle Press who have guided and sustained me through what has been a very challenging year. I am so proud to have my work published alongside so many amazing West Australian writers.

My sincere thanks to Liana Joy Christensen who read this manuscript when it was only twenty-three pages long. Her encouragement and thoughtful commentary enabled me to keep on writing with increased confidence and commitment.

My child Javier, himself a poet, also read this collection and their edits and wise engagement with my work made the poems richer and more redolent than they otherwise would have been. Thanks must also go to Javi for coming up with the title of the collection.

Finally, I must acknowledge the tremendous contribution made to this collection by my wife, Jo. She knows me and my work so intimately, and works with such insight and care that these poems owe much to her fierce and true reading and editing skills. I am eternally grateful to you, my love, for everything.

First published 2022 by
FREMANTLE PRESS

Fremantle Press Inc. trading as Fremantle Press
PO Box 158, North Fremantle, Western Australia, 6159
fremantlepress.com.au

Cover design and illustration by Holly Dunn, hollydunndesign.com

A catalogue record for this
book is available from the
National Library of Australia

ISBN 9781760991654 (paperback)
ISBN 9781760991661 (ebook)

lotterywest

Fremantle Press is supported by the Western Australian State Government through the Department of Cultural Industries, Tourism and Sport.

Fremantle Press respectfully acknowledges the Whadjuk people of the Noongar nation as the Traditional Owners and Custodians of the land where we work in Walyalup.